THE MYTH OF LIVING THE CHRISTIAN LIFE

REALLY ENJOYING THE CHRISTIAN LIFE INSTEAD OF JUST ENDURING IT

BY THE AUTHOR OF THE IDENTITY DRIVEN LIFE SERIES

CHRIS J. GREGAS

Individual or Small Group Study Guide

Contents

As with every study guide, there are some things that you need to keep in mind to maximize the study and see life change from it. Consider the following:

Please read the chapter before the study. I know this sounds insulting, but it is amazing how much we lose and how we can gain in our study just by either just showing up or by reading the chapter – maybe even twice!

Please pray before you study this material. Nothing in our life is solidified unless we allow God entrance and prayer throws open the door for God to be "in the house" why we talk about these life changing truths.

Don't be in any hurry to go through this material. In a perfect world, you could finish this study in 10 weeks or about 2.5 months. But doing the study justice will probably be closer to 4–5 months, so take your time and wrestle with these teachings.

Remind yourself that Satan hates for you to be a part of this study. He will do everything he can to minimize it, discourage you from being a part of it and giving you enough "good" reasons to not finish what you started. Don't give in to any of his nonsense. God will change you if you let Him through this study. Satan is well aware of that as well.

- *The Identity Driven Life: Why*
- *Knowing Who You Are Is Just as Important as Knowing Why You Are*
- *The Identity Driven Life – Small Group Study Guide*
- *The Identity Driven Life 2 – The Sequel*
- *The Identity Driven Life 2 – Small Group Study Guide*
- *Fearational: The Church in the Era of Covid-19*
- *The Healing Power of Gratitude*
- *25 Days of Christmas Devotional*
- *A Blockbuster Trade: Trade Satan's Lies for God's Truth*
- *A Blockbuster Trade: Trade Satan's Lies for God's Truth – Small Group Study Guide*
- *Blessings All Day the Throne Room*
- *Surviving the Grind Without Becoming the Powder: 365 Daily from Meditations to Encourage and Challenge Entrepreneurs and Sales Leaders*
- *The Myth of Living the Christian Life*

Study 1 – The Myth of Living the Christian Life

Myth :

*a traditional story, especially one concerning the early
history of a people or explaining some natural or social
phenomenon, and typically involving supernatural beings
or events. A widely held but false belief or idea.*

1. **What would you give or sacrifice to have inner peace
    and joy on an ongoing basis?**

2. **Why didn't God save you and then immediately
    transport you to Heaven that very hour He delivered
    you?**

Much of the Newer Testament centers around evil static in
the line and consistent drama concerning the ministry of
false teachers. Those who peddle lies and myths, hoping to

capture and enslave unsuspecting and illiterate believers. At the end of the day, we become the sum of what we believe and what we are willing to trust in. And if what we believe is not rooted in *truth*, we will be on a fast track that yields *spiritual and emotional upheaval.*

There is a debilitating myth when it comes to living the Christian life that has the Christian church worldwide by the scruff of the neck. It has not always been this way, but it certainly is the culture that affects the church presently. It is *man centered* in nature and it is *works centered* in its explanation and application. It is a scandal across the church that is long overdue in giving this the urgent attention it deserves.

Discuss or define **Christian Life Myth #1:** *"Living the Christian life is solely or mostly - **up to us**."*

Discuss or define **Christian Life Myth #2:** *"Living the Christian life hoping to **improve** as a Christian."*

Discuss or define **Christian Life Myth #3:** *"The Christian life cannot be **enjoyed** so it is be **endured**."*

Discuss or define **Christian Life Myth #4:** *"The Christian life is really **hard work** and a **constant struggle** to succeed and advance."*

Discuss or define **Christian Life Myth #5:** *"The Christian life is all about - **letting go and letting God**."*

Discuss or define **Christian Life Myth #6:** *"We are just **a sinner saved by grace** and therefore we must do the best we can to live for Christ."*

Discuss or define **Christian Life Myth #7** *"God truly helps those who **help themselves**."*

3. *How many of these "myths" have you bought in to? How many have you come to believe are a major part of your Christian life?*

The Results of Believing Myths and Lies?

4. **Why and how does believing myths and lies choke out the truth in our lives.**

5. **Is it any Christian's desire "deep down" to follow the enemy of their souls with a carefree and happy attitude?**

6. **Do you think being ignorant or disinterested in living the Christian life to the fullest will effect your life here and your rewards there? Discuss.**

How should I then live?

Study 2 – Is It Either Or – Or Both And?

"The life of the believer is not in himself, but in his Lord: "He that has the Son has life; and he that has not the Son of God has not life." "I live," says the apostle Paul; "yet not I, but Christ lives in me;" and, writing to the Colossians, he says, "For you are dead, and your life is hidden with Christ in God." Just as this finger of mine lives because of its union with the head, and with the heart, and with the rest of my being where life is to be found, so do you and I live because we have been joined unto Christ. If there were no life in the stem, there would be no life in the branch. If the branch is severed from the vine, it has no life in itself."
-C.H. Spurgeon

1.   *Whose **responsibility** is it to act in the Christian life:*
     Christ or ours?

*"Come to me, all of you who are weary and
burdened, and I will give you rest. Take up my
yoke and learn from me, because I am lowly and
humble in heart, and you will find rest for your
souls. For my yoke is easy and my burden is light."
(Matthew 11:28-30 – CSB)*

Discuss these verses. What was Jesus saying here?

Come to *Me* – period without pause or hesitation.

Why?

*Because you are emotionally and spiritually tired and
overly burdened.*

*Because He is the One who can truly give you real and
lasting spiritual rest and inner peace.*

*Because you can learn from someone who is totally humble
and perfectly submissive to the Father - and what a lesson
that might be.*

*Because my teaching and way of life is much more freeing
than anything the world offers or educates you with.*

Prayer: "Father, I come to you and your Son and ask for your rest and peace. I pray you lift this burden of doing and striving off of my shoulders and take away my desire to work to exhaustion. Allow me to sit in Your presence and let You do all of the spiritual work. I pray you mold me into Your image, instilling in me a restful spirit. Let me radiate Your peace onto others, even in the midst of chaos, and show me how to walk down the path of rest that has at the end You. In Jesus Name - Amen."

Discuss what these verses seem to imply about the Christian life.

Therefore, my beloved, as you have always obeyed, so now, not only as in my presence but much more in my absence, work out your own salvation with fear and trembling, for it is God who works in you, both to will and to work for his good pleasure. **(Phil. 2:12-13)**

2.   *What does it mean that - "God gives the birds their food, but He doesn't throw it into their nests."*

The Christian life can never work powerfully without us having a proper marriage (partnership) with our Groomsman, Jesus Christ. Since we are His bride, we must know that He is rooting for us to succeed and He is ever desirous for us to be in perfect precision with His work around the world. But that will never happen if we fail to realize what Christ's work is and what ours is. What we are responsible for and what only He can pull off by His omnipotent hand.

How should I then live?

"We think of the Christian life as a 'changed life' but it is not that. What God offers us is an 'exchanged life,' a 'substituted life,' and Christ is our substitute within." -Watchman Nee, The Normal Christian Life

1. Discuss what it means when we say, "experiencing the new birth is a divine miracle."

2. Read 2 Cor. 5:17. Does this verse describe a CHANGED life or an EXCHANGED life?

Watchman Nee writes, "Isaiah 61:3 says, *"To appoint unto them that mourn in Zion, to give unto them beauty for ashes, the oil of joy for mourning, the garment of praise for the spirit of heaviness; that they might be called trees of righteousness, the planting of the LORD, that he might be glorified."* God's way is the way of replacement. God does not change the ashes. Rather, He replaces the ashes with a headdress. He does not change the mourning. Rather, He replaces the mourning with gladness. ***God's way is never to change, but to exchange.***"

3. *Discuss what Nee means. How does this affect your Christian life?*

When you became a believing sinner, a great exchange took place. Jesus Christ took your place and died for you on the cross. All of your sins were placed upon Jesus Christ, and He died in your stead. In that great transaction, Christ willingly took all your sins and guilt, and in "exchange" you received His righteousness as your eternal position in Christ.

Helpful Illustration…

If I take a 3x5 card and place it between the pages in my Bible that card becomes a part of my Bible. Regardless of where I take my Bible it goes with it. If I lay my Bible down somewhere that 3x5 card goes with it. If I lose my Bible, I lose the 3x5 card. The card is now a part of my Bible. In the same way, I am now so identified with Jesus Christ through His death and resurrection, and the new life the Holy Spirit has imparted to me that I am in Christ. I go with Him wherever He goes.

How should I then live?

Study 4 – Sin Conscious or Saint Conscious?

"Therefore, do not let sin reign in your mortal body, that you should obey it in its desires. And do not present your members as instruments of unrighteousness to sin but present yourselves to God as being alive from the dead, and your members as instruments of righteousness to God. For sin shall not have dominion over you, for you are not under law but under grace."
-Romans 6:12-14

The Christian life and the work of Christ on our behalf can be reduced to this simple summary:

*God has **[past tense]** saved us from the **penalty** of sin – the biblical term for that is being **justified**; being declared perfectly righteous before God in Christ.*

*God is saving **[present tense]** us from the **power** of sin –the biblical term for that is sanctification; being increasingly set apart for God's use.*

*God will **[future tense]** save us from the **presence** of sin – the Bible describes as the process of glorification; being seated in the heavenlies with Christ in actuality forever.*

1. ***Discuss or think about what I ask, "do we in this world (and even in the church) even know what "sin" is anymore?"***

2. ***How do you presently defeat sin and temptation in your life? How does it really happen so you and I can see spiritual victory in our lives and not just talk about it?***

3. *Discuss what it means to be consistently "sin conscious. Is being sin conscious helpful or hurtful to the child of God?*

4. *Discuss repentance. What does it mean and does a Christian need to practice it?*

5. *Based on what you read in the book, how many times does God call us, we who are His children, "sinners" in the New Testament?*

6. *Discuss the statement, "Saints are born not made." How does that square with what how the world defines - sainthood?*

7. *Who were the fleshliest, misguided, childish and immature believers in the New Testament? (Read I Corinthians 1:1-3 and discuss)*

"Called to be saints" is what Paul says. That is who they were and that is **who we are** if Jesus knows us. That is in fact our truest spiritual identity. Sinners yes but that is not what we are by position or standing **now** that we have come out of spiritual darkness into the light of Christ! (Col. 1:13) We are saints of the living God and because we are, we can be "set apart" to do the good things that God has for us. Do not miss the order!

How should we then live?

*"If Christ is in us, what will be the consequences?
Why, He will put us aside entirely. The I in us will
go. We will say, "Not I, but Christ." Christ
undertakes our battles for us. Christ becomes
purity and grace and strength in us."*
-A.B. **Simpson**

1. **What does Paul mean when he says in Romans 13:14, *"But put on the Lord Jesus Christ, and make not provision for the flesh, to fulfill its desires."***

2. *The bumper sticker "Jesus is my co-pilot" may be a well-intentioned sentiment, but it does not have any scriptural support? Why or why not?*

3. *Follow-up Question: If you were driving a car, would Jesus be in the passenger seat or the drivers seat?*

An Intimate Look at Galatians 2:20

I have been crucified with Christ. It is no longer I who live, but Christ who lives in me. And the life I now live in the flesh I live by faith in the Son of God, who loved me and gave himself for me. (ESV)

4. Discuss or think about what this verse actually implies to your life and walk with Christ?

"I have been crucified with Christ,"

*The **first thing** we notice about this phrase is that it is – past tense. "I have been."*

In other words, it has been already accomplished with continuing results. That is how the original language (Greek) translates it. It is not something that is going to happen or even needs to happen as if we ourselves had a hand in seeing this happen. It is has happened and it was done by God – once for all, for every believing sinner.

The **second** *thing* is we died spiritually. It says we have been **"crucified"**.

In **Romans 6**, Paul tells us that the same way and at the same time Jesus was crucified, we were, spiritually speaking. In other words, when Jesus died, we died. Our old self (*in my case, the old Chris Gregas)* that who we were before we came into a new relationship with God through Christ, was, once for all, put to death so that the old us would be rendered powerless spiritually speaking.

Lastly, we have died – ***"in and with Christ."***

We did not die ourselves. We died in and with Christ. Which means that all that He did to die and be buried only to rise to newness of life is our inheritance as well. **(Romans 6:3-13)** Paul says that we died to sin once and now we live to God.

"It is no longer I who live,"

First, ***we as Christian's no longer live as it relates to our old self.***

Paul is not saying we do not live anymore but the radius and scope of our living is no longer the way it used to be in our unsaved state. *Why?* Because our old self has been once and for all – crucified and put to death by the cross work of Jesus Christ. What does that mean? That the old Chris Gregas, B.C. (before Christ) is dead and gone. There is nothing I can do to bring him back. When I truly realize what I was before I knew Christ, why would I ever want to bring him back?

Second, ***our Christian life is not to be lived by our own strength or in the power of our old self or life.***

In other words, the way we lived life before Christ can never work or be acted on after we come to know Christ. It does not work simply because what was the standard before is not the standard now. In fact, that is what Paul says in Romans 6:14 when he writes, *"You are no longer under the [rule] law but under [the rule] of grace."* Grace is always a higher standard than the law which means there is more responsibility on us because we have ***Someone*** else who is able and willing to live this life, we call Christian. That Someone is of course, Jesus Christ.

5. ***What advantage is to live the Christian life in our own strength?***

"but Christ who lives in me,"

"Paul thinks of himself as having become so closely identified with Christ that Christ dominates his whole experience." ...he thinks no longer of carnal living pursuing the desires and impulses of the self, but a new kind of living, a faith life." **-Donald Guthrie**

"There is no halfway life in Christ because there is no Christ who is halfway alive. There is only life in Christ and death apart from Him. There is only shame and guilt and sorrow and fear, or else all of that is crucified with Christ and we live because He, being fully alive, lives in us." **-Toby Sumpter**

6. *Think and meditate on the phrase again, "Christ who lives in me." What do you think the Holy Spirit had in mind when he moved Paul to write this?*

"And the life I now live in the flesh I live by faith in the Son of God,"

The writer says, *"What we have here is a remarkably interesting phrase. It is translated "live by faith in the Son of God" but that is a poor translation indeed. Other translations say (which seem to sum up with the original language conveys)* **The faith OF the Son of God.** *We might say we understand what it means to live* **BY** *our faith* **IN** *the Son of God. But this verse suggests something else: We are to live* **IN** *the faith* **OF** *the Son of God."*

7. *What is this faith OF the Son of God, and how does one live IN it?*

Andrew Wommack points out, *"Paul did not say that he lived by faith IN the Son of God but by the faith OF the Son of God. The measure of faith that Paul had was the same measure that Jesus had.*

"who loved me and gave himself for me,"

8. *What does it mean to you for Christ to give Himself FOR you?*

"The work of God does not mean so much man's work for God, as God's own work through man." - **Hudson Taylor**

How should we then live?

Study 6 - What the Devil Doesn't Want You to Know

"There is no neutral ground in the universe; every square inch, every split second, is claimed by God and counter-claimed by Satan." -C.S. Lewis

1. How do sharpen your "spiritual axe"? When was the last time you sharpened your ax?"

We must follow Paul's example and *not be ignorant of Satan's devices* (2 Corinthians 2:11). This means we must understand the devil's tricks and traps and examine how he uses his key weapons in individually targeted ways to attack each of us. Let us be reminded of a few important things as we talk about Satan and his desire to see you fail in your Christian walk.

First, **Satan is a liar and a murderer. (John 8:44)**

Snap out of it. Satan is trying to destroy you and the ones you love – and love you. Do not let that happen!

Second, **Satan wants us to be entrapped so we will do his will.**

2 Timothy 2:26 says, "*and they may come to their senses and escape from the snare of the devil, having been held captive by him **to do his will**.*" The amazing thing is that even as believers in Christ, we can be captured and caged by the devil to work for him and spread his poison.

Third, **the devil is always desirous to get us separated from our life, Jesus Christ.**

When we are deceived in to believing that we can go it alone or feel empowered to just ask Jesus to come along for the ride, we are asking for spiritual trouble and heartache in waves. Lone Ranger Christians are always in way over their heads.

What Diablos Does Not Want You to Know...

Satan does not want you to know...

"Without Christ, you can do nothing."

1. *What does that mean to our activity in the Christian life?*

We must always remember that - *We bear spiritual fruit; we do not produce fruit.* In our Christian walk, we must live by this maxim: *With Jesus everything is possible and without Jesus, nothing is possible.* Our lives must be Christ-sufficient and not self-sufficient. This is the only way to bear lasting fruit that will bear dividends into eternity.

Satan does not want you to know...

"Jesus is the only One that can live the Christian life successfully."

2.   What does that mean?

There is only one person who has ever lived the Christian life successfully or sinlessly and that is – *the One who bears the Christian name – Christ!* Contrary to what many of us have been taught, the Christian life is not only difficult to live – it is impossible to live.

Satan does not want you to know...

"Through Christ, who strengthens me, I can do all things..."

3.   What does this verse mean to you?

"This phrase might sound familiar to you. It is the right way *(the proper Greek construction of the verse)* to quote Philippians 4:13. And in quoting it this way, it takes on a different emphasis and power. The devil would love you to read this verse in a way that most of us, in fact, actually read it and believe it. What is that? It is the emphasis on **"I"** can do all things. *"I can do all things"* becomes more about us and how God comes along side us to perform the work instead of us partnering with God as He performs His work. One says that Christ is a willing participant to what we are engaged in. The other (*which is the biblical teaching*) says that we, in any situation we find ourselves in, are actively involved in finding out what Christ is doing and joining Him in His work. In this model, Christ is the One who is running the show allowing us by His grace, to join Him in what He is doing as He advances His great and widening kingdom – one soul at a time." -CJG

Satan certainly does not want you to know…

"that He [Satan] was, once for all, spiritually defeated by Christ, on the cross and through His resurrection."

Do you want scriptural proof?

And you, who were dead in your trespasses and the uncircumcision of your flesh, God made alive together with him, having forgiven us all our trespasses, by canceling the record of debt that stood against us with its legal demands. This he set aside, nailing it to the cross. ***He disarmed the rulers and authorities and put them to open shame, by triumphing over them in him.*** **(Colossians 2:13-15 - ESV)**

Since therefore the children share in flesh and blood, he himself likewise partook of the same things, ***that through death he might destroy the one who has the power of death, that is, the devil,*** *and deliver all those who through fear of death were subject to lifelong slavery.* **(Hebrews 2:14-15 – ESV)**

Whoever makes a practice of sinning is of the devil, for the devil has been sinning from the beginning. ***The reason the Son of God appeared was to destroy the works of the devil.*** *No one born of God makes a practice of sinning, for God's seed abides in him; and he cannot keep on sinning, because he has been born of God.* **(1 John 3:8-9 – ESV)**

When I saw him, I fell at his feet as though dead. But he laid his right hand on me, saying, "Fear not, I am the first and the last, and the living one. I died, and behold I am alive forevermore, and I have the keys of Death and Hades. **(Revelation 1:17-18 – ESV**

"As long as we are seeking our worth in anything and everything but the gospel of God's grace, we will keep seeking and keep wearing ourselves out in the process. But in Christ's finished work is ultimate and eternal validation. And ultimate and eternal rest." **-Tullian Tchividjian, It Is Finished: 365 Days of Good News**

Defining the Finished Work of Jesus Christ

1. How would you define the "finished work of Jesus Christ?"

2. Name some truths of what the scriptures declare Jesus to be?

"And this is eternal life, that they know you, the only true God, and Jesus Christ whom you have sent. I glorified you on earth, having accomplished the work that you gave me to do. And now, Father, glorify me in your own presence with the glory that I had with you before the world existed." **(John 17:3-5)**

Have this mind among yourselves, which is yours in Christ Jesus, who, though he was in the form of God, did not count equality with God a thing to be grasped, but emptied himself, by taking the form of a servant, being born in the likeness of men. And being found in human form, he humbled himself by becoming obedient to the point of death, even death on a cross. **(Phil. 2:5-8)**

"For by him all things were created, in heaven and on earth, visible and invisible, whether thrones or dominions or rulers or authorities—all things were created through him and for him." **(Colossians 1:16)**

3. What do these verses reveal MOST about Jesus Christ?

The Chalcedon Creed declares:

1. Jesus has two natures – He is God and man.
2. Each nature is full and complete — He is fully God and
fully man.
3. Each nature remains distinct.
4. Christ is only one person.
5. Things that are true of only one nature are nonetheless true of the person of Christ.

Here is the **CONCLUSION.** ***Jesus is the only one that holds the power and authority to offer freely eternal salvation to the elect.***

There are ***two basic questions*** that remain.

The ***first question*** Jesus Himself asked His disciples. *"But what about you?" he asked. "Who do you say I am?"* **(Matthew 16:15)**

The ***second question*** Jesus posed to Pontius Pilate, *"What shall I do, then, with Jesus who is called Christ?"* **(Matthew 27:22)**

In the final analysis, we do not stand in our work or accomplishments - but in His and His alone. I love what the great prince of preachers, Charles Haddon Spurgeon had to say about this *"Conquering Savior"* one day in the pulpit that he mounted weekly for several years.

"Christ was a man of war, our glorious Joshua was he; he had come to gird on the sword, to invest him with the armor, and to go out and battle with Satan, with sin, and with hell. It was a terrible conflict, it was a fearful battle, but he girded himself for the mighty and the solemn work, and he completed it, he finished it. He met his foes on the battlefield, confronted all his enemies, and on the cross, he destroyed — he divested death of its sting, triumphed over Satan, the grave, and hell, and as he expired exclaimed, "It is finished!" Oh, what a sublime conflict was that my brethren, when the Captain of our salvation met single-handed and overcame the powers of darkness, fought the fight, won the victory, and died, saying "It is finished!"

What a spring of comfort flows from it to the true believer amid his innumerable failures, flaws, and imperfections. What service do you perform, what duty do you discharge of which you can say, "It is finished?" Alas! not one; your service is imperfect, your obedience is incomplete, your love is fluctuating, yea, upon it all are visible the marks of human defilement and defect. But here is the work which

God most delights in, "finished." "Ye are complete in him." Turn you, then, your eye of faith out of yourself, and off of all your own doings, and deal more immediately, closely, and obediently with the finished work of Immanuel. Come away from your fickle love, from your weak faith, from your little fruitfulness, from your uneven walk, from all your short-comings and imperfections, and let your eye of faith repose where God's eye of complacent love reposes, on the finished work of Jesus."

How Should we then live?

Study 8 - Beggar or Appropriator: Which Are You?

A ***beggar*** is one who looks for favor from others, not because he has worked for such a blessing but simply because he feels entitled to receive and be blessed. The beggar is one who is unaware of his own benefits and abilities and has become dependent on everyone else for their success and happiness.

An ***appropriator*** or the one who applies the benefits that are available is one who does not spend senseless hours and time trying to receive that which has and is already available to them. They simply live out what is in fact is theirs and in front of them. No begging, only enjoying what is in fact theirs by grace.

Understanding How to Appropriate and Enjoy What Is Ours in Christ

"Now <u>faith</u> is the assurance (title deed, confirmation) of things hoped for (divinely guaranteed), and the evidence of things not seen [the conviction of their reality—<u>faith</u> comprehends as fact what cannot be experienced by the physical senses]." (Hebrews 11:1 – Amplified Version)

1. ***What role does FAITH have in us appropriating all that is ours in Christ?***

The ***riches of God*** have been made available to us in Christ, yet most of us shrink back from receiving all that God eagerly wishes to place in our hands. The riches of God cannot help us until we open the door of our hearts.

Breaking Down – James 4:8

"Submit yourselves therefore to God. Resist the devil, and he will flee from you."

Step 1: *Submit to God.*

2.   *What does it really mean to submit to God?*

How does the word or the action to submit to God allow us to appropriate the finished work of Christ in our lives?

First, ***we must understand that this is a COMMAND to be followed and obeyed.***

FYI - This is not just a suggestion or a good idea to be considered among many other options. It is command from God and as all other commands are to be obeyed, so this edict is to be accepted and obeyed as well. God does not require us to submit because He is a tyrant, but because He is a loving Father, and He knows what is best for us.

Secondly, *submission to God is not a whim experience but it is a lifestyle approach.*

As we consider what it means to living the abundant life that is our heritage in Christ, we must fully believe that not only is submission to God a command, but it is logical, and a lifestyle walk that is not perfect but consistent.

Step #2: *Resist the devil.*

3. *What does it mean to - resist the devil?*

> *Be sober-minded; be watchful. Your adversary the devil prowls around like a roaring lion, seeking someone to devour. [9] <u>Resist him</u>, firm in your faith, knowing that the same kinds of suffering are being experienced by your brotherhood throughout the world. -I Peter 5:8-9 ESV*

Submit and arrange ourselves under the control and sway of God as consistently as we can.

Resist the devil and not allow him to control our minds and our flesh in any form or fashion.

> *"The sons of the King do not conduct themselves like the devil's beggars."*
> *—John MacArthur*

Result: *The devil will flee/run. [from you]*

4. What does it mean that the "devil will run?"

The *formula* for spiritual victory is crystal clear. The *formula* for casting out the beggarly attitude that is so easily is adopted by the most ardent Christian is simple:

Submit to God - Resist the Devil = He will run and leave

How Should we then live?

Study 9 - The Mortal Combat Between your Flesh and the Holy Spirit?

"The one who sows to please his flesh, from the flesh will reap destruction; but the one who sows to please the Spirit, from the Spirit will reap eternal life." **-Galatians 6:8**

1.   What does it mean when we say – "Self is useless in the eyes of God."

Hint: Look at Romans 7:18.

What is self or the flesh exactly?

Self can be best described as the absence of God in our lives while we do what we do. It is us doing the work of God either in our own strength or blindly believing that "God is my partner, and I can handle any situation." Is that true? It is using our fleshly mind to perform the work of God or even more disturbing, it is thinking that it is up to us to accomplish the work of Christ with His assistance. No doubt Christ is there but He is more of a ***"helper"*** rather than our ***"Life"*** (Col. 3:4) and the one who is the wind beneath our wings. (Gal. 2:20) -CJG

You and I as believers in Christ have ***two important things in common.***

First, *we both have a flesh, that which the Bible calls, "this body of sin" that we are saddled with from birth to death. It is the playground of Satan and his demons and it is the very landscape that wreaks havoc in the Christian's life in great measure.*

Second, *all Christian's have in common is that we have all been gifted with the presence of God the Holy Spirit that*

takes residence within us the moment we are born again of the Spirit.

The Old Nature, the Flesh and The Holy Spirit in the Christian Life

THE OLD NATURE.

2. *Do you and I as believers **still have** an old nature or a sinful nature? Do you and I as believers have **TWO** natures within us?*

3. Discuss Romans 6:6 - **We know that our old self was crucified with him in order that the body of sin might be brought to nothing, so that we would no longer be enslaved to sin. (ESV)**

*#1: We still have or possess a sin nature living within us.
that conflicts with the new nature. In other words, we
have two natures equally at battle within.*

*#2: We no longer have a sin nature within us, but we have
the flesh left to battle with the Spirit. The old nature is
gone, the flesh is left and that is what causes us to sin as we
as believers - surrender to it.*

*#3: We still have the sin nature in us, but it has been
rendered powerless in our lives. In other words, the "right
and authority" of the old nature has been broken and we
no longer must serve it.*

Q. Which one do you believe is the scriptural teaching?

4. *Have you or are you learning to say NO to sin and
    YES to Christ? What is the PROOF?*

THE FLESH.

When the Bible refers to the ***"flesh"*** it is just not talking
about the wrapping that keeps our muscles from falling off
our bones. It is speaking of our evil makeup: ***those desires,
patterns and lines of thinking, those behaviors and
attitudes that are deep within in us that are bent away
from God.***

Reminders Concerning the Flesh

First, we need to know that - *our sinful flesh has nothing **good** to offer us.*

Romans 7:18 states, *"I know that nothing good lives in me, that is, in my flesh…"*

Secondly, *God's purpose was and is to never **improve** the flesh but to subject it to crucifixion.*

The sinful flesh of a man or a Christian cannot be improved upon or renovated and reformed. **Why?** Because it is terribly tainted with sin and sinful patterns. God could have chosen to **reform** it, but in His great wisdom, He chose to be subject to **crucifixion** instead!

Galatians 5:24 - *"those who belong to Christ Jesus have crucified the **FLESH** with its passions and desires."*

Thirdly, *the flesh is **hostile** to God and His will.*

Romans 8:5-7 reveals, *"For those who are according to the flesh set their minds on the things of the flesh, but those who are according to the Spirit, the things of the Spirit. [6] For the mind set on the flesh is death, but the mind set on the Spirit is life and peace, [7] because the mind set on the flesh is **hostile** toward God; for it does not subject itself to the law of God, for it is not even able to do so."*

Fourthly, *those who live by the flesh **cannot** please God.*

Romans 8:8 states, *"and those who are in the flesh **cannot** please God."* (NASB)

**5. *Is pleasing Christ your overriding goal in life? If not,
why not?***

Fifthly, *the flesh is in **direct opposition** with the Holy
Spirit.*

Galatians 5:16-17, *"But I say, walk by the Spirit, and you
will not gratify the desires of the flesh. For the desires of
the flesh are **against** the Spirit, and the desires of the Spirit
are **against** the flesh, for these are **opposed** to each other,
to keep you from doing the things you want to do."*

Sixthly, *we must give no **authority** to the flesh in our lives.*

Romans 13:13-14, *"Let us behave decently, as in the
daytime, not in orgies and drunkenness, not in sexual
immorality and debauchery, not in dissension and jealousy.
Rather, clothe yourselves with the Lord Jesus Christ, and
do not think about how to gratify the desires of the sinful
flesh."*

Peter writes, *"Dear friends, I urge you, as aliens and
strangers in the world, to abstain from sinful desires, which
war against your soul."* **(I Peter 2:11)**

THE HOLY SPIRIT.

Summary:

In **Romans 6**, Paul develops the idea of our spiritual
identity as it relates to Christ's death and resurrection. He

lets us know that God has not only freed us from *the penalty and guilt of sin* but more practically, He has freed us and is freeing us from *the very power of sin* that so easily seeks to master us.

In **Romans 7**, Paul relates to the Roman Christians the power and potential domination of our own sinful flesh. Self or our flesh in its many forms seeks to control us from sunup to sundown. Paul says, what we want to do, we cannot seem to regularly do. What we do not want to do, we find ourselves doing and even longing to do in increasing measure. It is a bad scene all the way around.

But, in God's wisdom, it is not the end of the story. The story is just plain incomplete without **Romans 8** and the work of the Holy Spirit in our lives. The Spirit in essence is the ***exclamation point*** to what Paul discusses in chapters 6 and 7. The Holy Spirit is the power and means to apply the truths of both chapters. He is the answer to sin, self and the cross and how we step into spiritual victory which by the way - ***is applied effectively only through the Holy Spirit's working.***

The Holy Spirit's Work in The Christian Life

When the Holy Spirit is free to dominate the life of a Christian – there you will find divine authority and great spiritual influence. That has nothing to do with denominational flavor or religious belief or even what you say or believe about the Holy Spirit. It is all about His rightful and healthy influence in our lives.

Summary of the Spiritual Man or Woman

*The spiritual man has **accepted** Christ as his - Savior.*
*The spiritual man has **yielded** to Christ as his - Lord.*
*The spiritual man has **appropriated** Christ as his Life.*

6.   Has there ever been a time when you asked God the Holy Spirit to fill you with Himself? To pour out and over you His mighty power to overflowing?

How Should we then live?

"Do you think all Christians die happy? Not on your life! Some of them die as miserable sinners. Why? Because they've misused their time and wasted their lives. Many of you have laid dying on a hospital bed and prayed, "Lord, if you would only spare me, I'll do this, that, or the other." Well, have you done it?" **-Leonard Ravenhill**

1. What do you think of Ravenhill's quote?

One of these days, all of us who are saved are going to give account for our lives *after* we were saved. *After* is the key word.

"For we will all stand before the judgment seat of God; for it is written, "As I live, says the Lord, every knee shall bow to me, and every tongue shall confess to God." So, then each of us will give an account of himself to God." *(14:10-12 ESV)*

"So, whether we are at home or away, we make it our aim to please him. For we must all appear before the judgment seat of Christ, so that each one may receive what is due for what he has done in the body, whether good or evil. Therefore, knowing the fear of the Lord, we persuade others." **(2 Cor. 5:9-11)**

"For no one can lay a foundation other than that which is laid, which is Jesus Christ. Now if anyone builds on the foundation with gold, silver, precious stones, wood, hay, straw each one's work will become manifest, for the Day will disclose it, because it will be revealed by fire, and the fire will test what sort of work each one has done. If the work that anyone has built on the foundation survives, he will receive a reward. If anyone's work is burned up, he

will suffer loss, though he himself will be saved, but only as through fire." (ESV)

2. The great statesman Daniel Webster was once asked, "What is the greatest thought that can occupy a man's mind? He replied: "My accountability to God".

What are your thoughts about Webster's statement?

3. Are you ready for your "final exam"? If not, why not? Discuss with one another.

How should we then live?

- The Identity Driven Life: Why
- Knowing Who You Are Is Just as Important as Knowing Why You Are
- The Identity Driven Life – Small Group Study Guide
- The Identity Driven Life 2 – The Sequel
- The Identity Driven Life 2 – Small Group Study Guide
- Fearational: The Church in the Era of Covid-19
- The Healing Power of Gratitude
- 25 Days of Christmas Devotional
- A Blockbuster Trade: Trade Satan's Lies for God's Truth
- A Blockbuster Trade: Trade Satan's Lies for God's Truth – Small Group Study Guide
- Blessings All Day the Throne Room
- Surviving the Grind Without Becoming the Powder: 365 Daily from Meditations to Encourage and Challenge Entrepreneurs and Sales Leaders
- The Myth of Living the Christian Life